MW00396078

Pro Football Hall of Fame
The Story Behind the Dream

by Barney Brantingham

Produced for the Pro Football Hall of Fame by Sequoia Communications Inc.

Design by Nanette Boyer. Edited by Richard Lane.

Copy edited by Shannon Clevenger. Typeset by TypeStudio.

All photography from the Pro Football Hall of Fame archives except the following:

John E. Biever/NFL Photos: 7
Malcolm Emmons/NFL Photos: 16
James Flores/NFL Photos: 5, 57
Robert Shaver/NFL Photos: 21
Carl Skalak/NFL Photos: 33
Tony Tomsic/NFL Photos: 2, 17, 32, inside back cover

Library of Congress   88-061324
Printed in Hong Kong   ISBN 0-917859-27-8

Contents

Welcome to the Hall of Fame

William "Pudge" Heffelfinger, a gentle giant and former football All-America at Yale, had a dicey decision to make in the bruising, flying wedge formation days of late 1892. He could keep playing amateur games for expense money or risk his status by pocketing $500 to play a grudge game in Pittsburgh.

Professional football was born November 12, 1892 when Heffelfinger took the money and played. And made history. Heffelfinger, who won his reputation by breaking up flying wedges, was worth the $500. After making one smashing tackle he picked up a

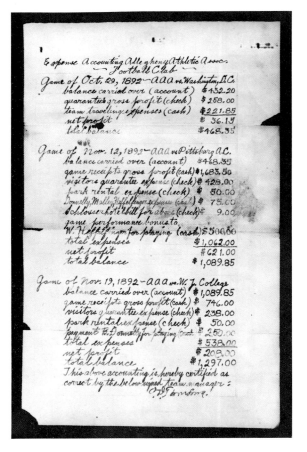

fumble and ran for the day's only score. Thanks to him, the Allegheny Athletic Association beat bitter archrival Pittsburgh Athletic Club, 4-0. Touchdowns were worth only four points then.

Professional football's birth certificate — the yellowed expense sheet recording the $500 — now hangs in the Pro Football Hall of Fame, in Canton, Ohio.

Why was Canton chosen for the Hall of Fame in the early 1960s? Because while pro football was born in Pennsylvania it soon fell into decline there and the Ohio region around Canton became the cradle. Canton was a hotbed of early grid-mania. The famed Canton Bulldogs became a power-house when the legendary Jim Thorpe, then the greatest name in American sports, joined them in 1915. And the first successful pro football league — now the NFL — was formed in Canton in 1920.

Pro football was a chaotic sport in those grass-roots days. "It was a rough game played by rough men, in small towns for small crowds," as one official put it. And for small money, too. Teams were born, blazed like comets, then fizzled out. Players hopscotched from team to team, virtually from week to week and often under assumed names. There were no set schedules.

Something had to be done, and it was done in Canton on September 17, 1920.

The man who made sports history with a $500 payday, "Pudge" Heffelfinger, above left, became America's first professional football player in 1892. The expense sheet showing a $500 payment to Heffelfinger for a grudge game in Pittsburgh, above, was dubbed pro football's "birth certificate."

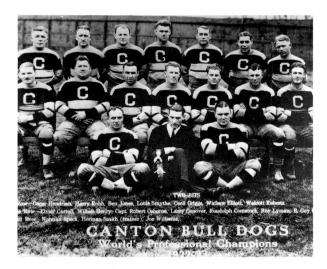

CANTON BULL DOGS
World's Professional Champions
1922

Manager Ralph Hay of the Canton Bulldogs called a meeting of owners and coaches of 11 teams. They sat on the fenders and running boards of cars in Hay's Hupmobile auto agency in downtown Canton. "In two hours we created the American Professional Football Association," recalled George Halas, then player-coach of the Decatur, Illinois, Staleys, soon to become the mighty Chicago Bears.

Thorpe, a public idol since his Carlisle Institute football days and smashing track and field victories in the 1912 Olympics, was named president. The gifted runner, passer, kicker and punishing defensive back was also player-coach of the Canton Bulldogs.

In two years the fledgling APFA would be renamed the National Football League and the Staleys would become the Bears. The Canton Bulldogs were undefeated in 1922 and 1923, the first two-time champs in the young NFL's history. Even though Thorpe had moved on, the Bulldogs still featured three future Hall of Famers, Link Lyman, Guy Chamberlin and Pete "Fats" Henry. Henry, who tilted the scales at between 250 and 300 pounds in an era of light linemen, was sensitive about his weight. Yet he was so fast he often carried the ball in clutch situations for the Bulldogs. A great kicker, Henry set two NFL records, with a 94-yard punt and a 50-yard dropkick.

The legendary Jim Thorpe was the world's most celebrated athlete when he joined the Canton Bulldogs in 1915. In 1920 the Sac and Fox Indian, right and top photos, was named to head the American Professional Football Association, later renamed the National Football League. Thorpe had moved on when the 1922 Bulldogs, above, won the NFL championship, but three of those Bulldogs are also enshrined in the Hall of Fame.

Yet pro football failed to catch the national imagination until 1925, when the immortal open field runner Red Grange burst onto the scene. That fall, the "Galloping Ghost" leaped directly from headline stardom at the University of Illinois to join the Chicago Bears on a wildly successful barnstorming trip. One game in New York against the Giants drew an unheard of 73,000 fans.

Nearly 40 years after the historic 1920 huddle in Ralph Hay's showroom, Canton was galvanized by an electrifying headline in the Canton Repository newspaper: "Pro Football Needs a Hall of Fame and Logical Site is Here." The December 6, 1959 article was the starting gun for community action.

Canton civic pride quickly formed a modern-day flying wedge, and on September 7, 1963 the Pro Football Hall of Fame opened its doors with a flourish. Halas, Grange, Thorpe and 14 other pioneer grid greats became charter enshrinees.

Since then, millions of fans from every state and scores of foreign countries have visited the Hall of Fame. Every year since 1963 at least three of the thousands of men who played, coached or contributed through the years have been elected to pro football's pantheon of heroes. They're honored in Canton during "Football's Greatest Weekend," kicking off the NFL preseason.

Red Grange of Illinois created a sensation when he signed with the Chicago Bears in 1925. Leaping from the campus to the pros, he helped legitimize the struggling professional game. At left he keeps warm under a fur coat on the sidelines. Cathedral-like dome of the Pro Football Hall of Fame, above, shelters a bronze statue of Jim Thorpe. Exhibit at right shows the well-worn blanket Jim Thorpe wore as a Canton Bulldog. The mural photo was taken at the 1916 Canton-Columbus game. Bibbed uniform at right worn by Syracuse fullback Harry Mason in 1902 provided slight protection in those bruising days.

Walk into the Hall of Fame's entry rotunda and you're struck by the feeling of being in a cathedral-like shrine. Stained glass brightens the 52-foot-high dome that resembles a huge football. Directly beneath the dome is a seven-foot high statue of Jim Thorpe, shown twisting away from a tackler. In bronze as he was on the gridiron, Thorpe remains larger than life. Behind him is a graceful ramp, as perfect a spiral as Johnny Unitas ever threw, curving up to the exhibition hall.

Here in the rotunda professional football's colorful life is traced, chapter by vivid chapter, from pioneers like Pudge Heffelfinger to record-setting exploits of today's superstars. It's also pro football's attic, where helmets, cleats and jerseys hang next to nostalgic scrapbook photos.

Quick now, when and where was the first pro indoor game? Answer: 1902, in New York City's Madison Square Garden. On display is the complete uniform worn by fullback Harry Mason of the Syracuse Athletic Club, which beat three straight indoor opponents in the Garden.

Near it is the oldest football in the Hall of Fame, a battered pigskin dating to about 1895 and almost as round as a basketball. A few steps away a huddled figure on a bench wears Jim Thorpe's old red sideline blanket, emblazoned with a big white "C" for Canton Bulldogs. Thorpe's blanket was donated after being found wrapped around a jack in the back of a car. At the player's feet is dirt taken from the very Canton field where the Sac and Fox Indian played. A nearby display case holds Thorpe's frayed Carlisle sweater, donated by an Akron woman whose dog used it for a bed.

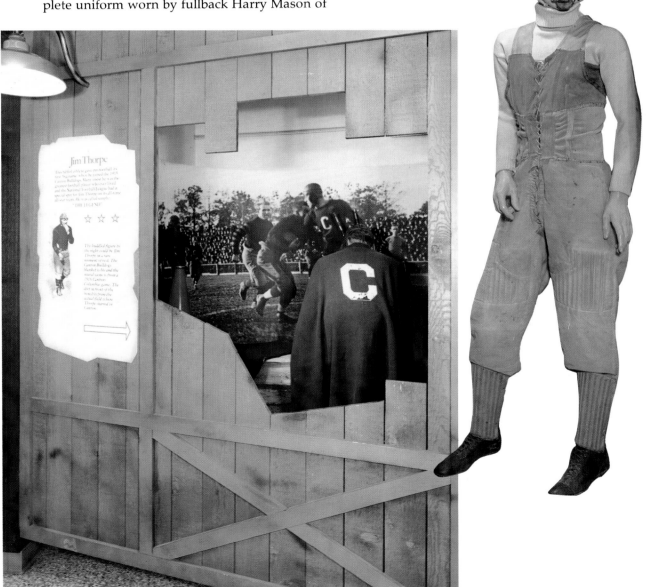

The thin leather helmets on display from that era seem more likely designed to conceal the identity of a collegian playing pro ball on Sunday than to protect his skull. Nor did the light, bibbed uniforms, flimsy shoulder pads and rubber nose-guards on display offer much protection in those bruising early days of the century.

A battered locker and an "Ernie Nevers' Eskimos" equipment trunk mark one of pro football's all-time feats of endurance. After headline-splashed heroics in the Rose Bowl, Stanford's triple-threat star played a home game with the Eskimos, then embarked with them on a marathon 28-game, 17,000-mile road trip in 1926. The Eskimos only had 15 players, and Nevers played all but 26 minutes of the entire 29-game schedule. He did all the kicking, most of the passing and ball carrying, played defense and coached to boot.

Sidelined once by an appendicitis attack, Nevers put himself in late in the game, threw a then-record 62-yard scoring pass and kicked the extra point to win, 7-6. Incredibly, the weary Eskimos ended the exhausting odyssey with 19 wins, only 7 losses and 3 ties. Iron Man Nevers left home weighing 210 pounds and returned 25 pounds lighter.

A gleaming trophy most visitors at first glance assume to be a silver football is a memento of the Great Pottsville Controversy of 1925. The Pottsville Maroons, located deep in the heart of the Pennsylvania coal-mining country, were outraged at being denied a championship they felt they'd earned. So their loyal fans simply declared them the 1925 NFL champions and made their own trophy out of hard anthracite coal.

One display shows Hall of Fame guard Danny Fortmann's uniform — not his Chicago Bears' blue and orange but the golden College All-Stars uniform he wore in the 1936 game. The pre-season Chicago College All-Star Game dreamed up by Chicago Tribune sports editor Arch Ward in 1934 pitted the cream of graduating seniors against the prior year's pro champs. The series, which delighted a nation of fans pulling for the underdog All-Stars, ended in 1976.

"Iron Man" Ernie Nevers, above, embarked on a marathon 28-game, 17,000-mile road trip with the Duluth, Minn., Eskimos in 1926. Gleaming trophy at right is made from polished coal, a memento of the Pottsville controversy of 1925. Denied a title, the Pottsville Maroons declared themselves champs and made their own trophy.

championships with his whiplike throwing arm, unmatched kicking ability and knack for picking off passes. In 1943 he won a triple crown in passing, punting and interceptions. On display in the rotunda is a plaster cast of Baugh's talented right hand along with his No. 33 jersey.

As World War II waned, Ohio's own Paul Brown was assembling the Cleveland Browns, a dynasty destined to dominate pro football's postwar years. Who would fill the shoes of the giant fullback he envisioned? Brown lined up Marion Motley, a 238-pound battering ram as fast and powerful as a young bull. During Motley's years starring at Canton's McKinley High School, Canton lost only three games. All were to neighboring rival Massillon High, then coached by none other than Paul Brown. Those same giant football shoes that Motley filled are on display in the rotunda. Nearby is the white helmet worn by the star Cleveland end Dante Lavelli and the uniform of Jim Brown, the all-time great Browns running back.

As pro football matured during the 1930s, the passing game opened up, making stars of light, elusive ends like Green Bay's Don Hutson and tricky, pass-happy quarterbacks like the Bears' Sid Luckman. Their jerseys — Hutson's 14 and Luckman's 42 — hang side by side in the rotunda.

Hutson, the "Alabama Antelope," combined dazzling speed with a brilliant array of moves. Teaming first with quarterback Arnie Herber, whose Packer greatcoat hangs in the Hall, he sparked pass-conscious Green Bay's glory years during a career from 1935 to 1945. Hardly a delicate shrinking violet despite his 180 pounds on a slim frame, Hutson played defensive end and safety in those rugged two-way days.

If Hutson was the first modern pro end, Luckman revolutionized quarterbacking. When Luckman arrived from little Columbia in 1939, George Halas had already installed the wide-open T-formation. The Bears began blitzing opponents with the man-in-motion, razzle-dazzle offense, and climaxed with a shocking 73-0 shutout of the proud Washington Redskins in the 1940 NFL Championship Game. And this was an era of low-scoring games. Soon other pro teams began discarding the brute-force single wing for the deceptive T. But only the Bears had Luckman, the slick magician. And he played defense, too.

"Slingin' Sammy" Baugh came off the Texas Christian campus in 1936. With Baugh as their triple-threat star, the Washington Redskins won

Hall of Fame exhibits show Ernie Nevers' heavy coat and one of the trunks his Duluth Eskimos used on their 1926 marathon road trip. The Eskimos only had 15 players and Nevers passed, kicked, ran, played defense and coached. Yet they returned from the exhausting trip with 19 wins.

Two other football shoes in the rotunda symbolize man's unquenchable desire and his ability to overcome adversity. One is the square-toed kicking shoe of Ben Agajanian, who lost all the toes on his kicking foot in a college elevator accident. Yet he went on to score 655 points kicking for nine different postwar teams. Another square-fronted shoe was worn by Tom Dempsey, who was born with only a partial right foot. While with the New Orleans Saints in 1970 he booted a record 63-yard field goal to beat the Detroit Lions in the closing seconds.

In 1956 a rail-thin "nobody" named Johnny Unitas, cut by the Pittsburgh Steelers in 1955 and found playing semi-pro ball for $6 a game, signed on as a Baltimore Colts backup quarterback. Thrust into a starting role by an injury, Unitas fired a touchdown pass against the Los Angeles Rams and launched one of the most outstanding feats in NFL history. Starting with that 1956 strike against the Rams, Unitas threw at least one TD pass in 47 straight games over four years. And his touchdown passes in the 1958 and 1959 title games weren't even counted. The rotunda displays his famous No. 19 uniform and the football he threw to pass the 40,000-yard career mark in 1973.

That big bass drum in the rotunda is the one the Baltimore marching band used between 1947 and 1965 to boom out after Colt victories. There's also a wristband with strange markings and a bizarre story behind it. When both Unitas and his backup were hurt in 1965, gutsy halfback Tom Matte quarterbacked the Colts into the playoffs, using plays written on a card and tucked into the wristband.

Dubbed "The Purple People Eaters" for the way they gobbled up ballcarriers and quarterbacks, the purple and white clad Minnesota Vikings' defensive line of the 1970s is remembered in the nearby Modern Era display. Here the full uniform of Vikings end Jim Marshall is on prominent display. Marshall, who spent a record 19 years with just one team, also established an NFL durability record of 282 consecutive games played.

In the 1980s a new generation of superstars took the spotlight and records crashed like runners hit by Bronko Nagurski. Their achievements found a place in the Hall of Fame spotlight even though no player is eligible for enshrinement until five years after he's hung up his cleats.

Eric Dickerson smashed Hall of Famer O.J. Simpson's season rushing mark in 1984 and set a new record of 2,105 yards. Dickerson's cleats, Los Angeles Rams jersey and the ball he carried won a berth in the rotunda. The Chicago Bears uniform Walter Payton wore in 1984 when he broke the great Jim Brown's career rushing record was also promptly put on display.

Tony Dorsett of the Dallas Cowboys sent his white lowcut shoes in 1983 to the Hall after he romped a record 99 yards for a touchdown against the Vikings. And speaking of overcoming adversity, the Cowboys only had 10 men on the field instead of 11.

Cut by the Steelers and discovered playing semi-pro ball at $6 a game, Johnny Unitas, opposite, went on to lead the Baltimore Colts during their glory days. Ben Agajanian lost the toes of one foot in an accident but became a kicking star using a square-toed right shoe, top left photo. Kicker Tom Dempsey, born with only a partial right foot, used an unusual shoe, inset left. He booted an astounding 63-yarder in 1970.

Big boom from Baltimore, this bass drum sounded off at Colts' games. Baltimore's marching band used it for more than 20 years. It's among the memorabilia that fills the rotunda exhibit room, above, at the Hall of Fame.

A Celebration of Excellence

*B*ill Dudley, everyone knew, was "too small and too slow" to play professional football. Yet he won two NFL rushing championships and a pass interception title with the Pittsburgh Steelers. And his bronze bust has a place in the Pro Football Hall of Fame.

Raymond Berry was a lowly 20th-round draft choice of the Baltimore Colts with little chance of making the team. He was no speedburner. Yet through determination Berry became an all-time great pass-catcher on the other end of Johnny Unitas' throws and a Hall of Famer.

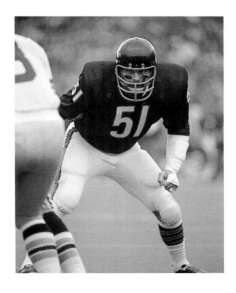

Emlen Tunnell broke his neck in college and was told he'd never play football again. After starring at Iowa he hitchhiked to New York to ask for a tryout with the Giants. There he won recognition in the great "Umbrella Defense" and a place in the Hall of Fame.

Ollie Matson came from a Texas Depression family so poor that as a boy he couldn't afford a football to play the game. Yet he refused to give up. Matson won an Olympic track medal, became an outstanding NFL runner and is enshrined in the Hall. His advice: "Don't quit."

A Hall of Famer must have that certain intangible quality that inspires him to overcome adversity, to excel. Call it "the right stuff." Call it true grit. But every man whose bronze bust stands in the Hall's gallery of enshrinees had it. Talent may be the engine of greatness, but dreams and dedication are the wings.

Former National Football League commissioner and Hall of Famer, Pete Rozelle, put it this way at one annual Hall of Fame enshrinement ceremony at Canton, Ohio: "Those who seem to be the most fierce competitors, perhaps making a great deal more of their physical abilities than they really have a right to, are those that are inducted in the Hall of Fame."

There are untold stories behind the blazing headlines made by every player in the Hall of Fame's twin enshrinement galleries. Many had to leap hurdles that would have tripped lesser men. Some, told they were too slow in the 40-yard dash, made up for it with 100-yard hearts.

At 5' 10" and 175 pounds (some say 5' 9" and 170) "Bullet Bill" Dudley was not big enough or fast enough to be an NFL halfback. He didn't even look like a football player, some said. He passed with a sidearm motion and booted field goals in an unorthodox way, without taking a step before kicking. Yet he twice won NFL rushing titles as an elusive runner for the Pittsburgh Steelers, Detroit Lions and Washington Redskins during the 1940s and 1950s. Dudley was also a sensational punt returner and a fine kicker. A 60-minute player, he was a bruising tackler who, in 1946, led the league in rushing, intercepting and punt returns.

"Raymond Berry was a 20th-round future draft choice in 1954 and was in reality given only a 50-50 chance of sticking when he joined the Colts in 1955," former Baltimore coach and Hall of Famer Weeb Ewbank told Berry's enshrinement audience.

An unheralded college player who hitchhiked to New York and asked the Giants for a job, Emlen Tunnell became part of the famed New York "Umbrella Defense." In 1952 the defensive star gained more yards through interceptions and kick returns than the NFL rushing champ did on offense.

"Those who seem to be the most fierce competitors, perhaps making a great deal more of their physical abilities than they really have a right to, are those that are inducted in the Hall of Fame."

—Pete Rozelle

Yet the Texan went on to form an unforgettable team with passer Johnny Unitas. In a 13-year Colt career, Berry fumbled only once. "Raymond had none of the characteristics you normally attribute to a great pass receiver," Ewbank said. "However, Raymond's pass patterns were so minutely perfected that he was almost unstoppable. I don't believe he had in his career 13 dropped balls. There were many years when he never dropped a ball. Raymond had many other things going for him: Unusual jumping ability, a pair of fantastic hands and a dogged sense of purpose that allowed him to become nothing less than the very best. He combined his dogged determination to succeed with the keen football mind that perfected the scientific approach to the art of pass receiving that was far ahead of his time."

End Ray Berry, right, fumbled only once in 13 years with the Baltimore Colts. But the Hall of Famer had to practice long hours to overcome his disadvantages: only average speed and size. A favorite target of passer John Unitas, he retired as the leading receiver in NFL history. Pete Rozelle, above, was named NFL Commissioner in 1960.

Joe Namath grew up poor in the steel mill town of Beaver Falls, Pennsylvania. The youngest of five children of divorced parents, Joe worked a variety of odd jobs to make ends meet. Then, after his college career at Alabama, the New York Jets pressed a reported $400,000 into his hand to pass the football for them. He became Broadway Joe, the toast of the town, wearing fur coats and dating glamorous women. To top it off, this brash kid from the new league "guaranteed" that the upstart AFL Jets would whip the NFL Baltimore Colts in Super Bowl III. And they did it, at least partly, on Namath's strong right arm, pulling off one of the greatest upsets in sports history. Pro football hasn't been the same since.

At his 1985 enshrinement Namath recalled the advice of his high school coach: "If you don't dream about it, it will never happen. But you can't just dream about it, you have to go out and make it happen. You have to work hard." Namath never forgot it.

One Hall of Famer never played on a championship team, was born into poverty but persevered and won a medal in the Olympics. No, not Jim Thorpe, but the speedy, powerful running back Ollie Matson. He was born in Trinity, Texas, in the Depression year of 1930. "When I was a youngster, I didn't have the money, my family didn't have the money to buy a football," he told the Canton audience at his 1972 enshrinement. "We had to take a can and wrap it up and we played with it. And as I look through the stadium today and see a number of young people I would like to say to you: Don't quit. Don't always ask for something without working for it. Because this life is not that way. You only get out of life what you put into it. And I put a lot into it." After winning a Bronze Medal in the 400-meter run in the

1952 Olympics, he told a friend, "When a man wants to do something and he has worked diligently, honestly and sincerely as I did, you can't beat him." In 1959 Matson hit the headlines when the Cardinals traded him to the Los Angeles Rams in exchange for nine — yes, nine — players.

Growing up on the streets of San Francisco, young O.J. Simpson was surrounded by temptations. One day his junior varsity high school coach caught him on his knees — not praying but shooting craps in the school bathroom. The coach took O.J. and his pals to the office, even though a suspension would mean that Simpson would miss the championship game, jeopardizing the coach's chance for promotion. Simpson, at his 1986 Hall of Fame enshrinement, repeated what the coach told him: "You've got to learn if you are ever going to be successful in this world, you are going to have to learn to accept the responsibilities for your actions." Simpson said he "began to realize that it really, really is secondary if you win or lose, it is how you play the game in life and on the field that matters."

Joe Namath, the Jets' brash young quarterback in the upstart American Football League, "guaranteed" a win over the Colts in Super Bowl III. Namath, opposite page, and the New York Jets quieted critics with one of the biggest upsets in sports history. O.J. Simpson, above and inset, a Hall of Famer who never made it to a Super Bowl, will go down in record books as one of the greatest running backs in pro history. He won four rushing titles with the Buffalo Bills and ran for a then-record 2,003 yards in 1973.

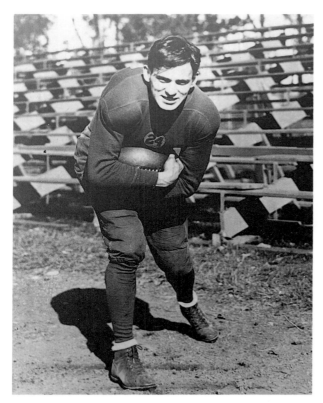

Johnny Unitas, a lowly ninth-round draft choice in 1955, didn't quit when the Pittsburgh Steelers cut him before the season started. He played semi-pro ball for $6 a game — and gave 110 percent. Baltimore Colt coach Weeb Ewbank heard about this sandlot quarterback with the slingshot arm and the rest, as they say, is history.

A tough player with old-fashioned ideals, Unitas wore a crew-cut and high-top black football shoes long after they were out of fashion. At his 1979 enshrinement, Unitas lauded his high school coach, James Carey. "He worked with me, talked with me, treated me like a son. I can always remember Max saying, 'When the going gets tough, the tough get going and that is what I expect out of you, 110 percent at all times.' I always tried to remember that and give 110 percent, whenever I was on the field or off. Regardless what it was, I felt that I was consistent and he always got 110 percent out of me."

Vince Lombardi was "a great leader of men; he had the ability to make men do more than they thought themselves capable of doing," Ohio Governor John J. Gilligan told the Hall of Fame audience at the Green Bay coach's 1971 enshrinement. Added Governor Gilligan: "Football is a team game and it involves self-discipline and self-sacrifice and the ability to work with others and that presumably is what our society is all about, not just the game of football."

Lombardi, who as an assistant helped build the great New York Giants of the 1950s, was 45 before he became a head coach. In 1959 he took over the floundering doormat Green Bay Packers. But from the first season, the fiery Italian never had a losing year. As Giants president Wellington Mara said at the ceremony: "Vince Lombardi did not invent professional football and he did not found the NFL, but he embellished both of them to a degree never surpassed and seldom, if ever, equalled. He made winners out of his players and losers out of his opponents."

Why, asked Carroll Rosenbloom, owner of the Baltimore Colts and then the Los Angeles Rams, "does one (person) prosper and another fail?" Speaking at the enshrinement of the Colts' great defensive end, Gino Marchetti, Rosenbloom said, "I think I have found the answer in Gino. Gino is credited with creating the crashing style of the modern defensive end play. The way he got to the passer has become legendary . . . not because God had given him a body better than others, but because he took what God gave him and got more from himself than he ever thought he would be able to give. The greatness that is in him will be with him for the rest of his life. An outstanding and unending commitment to excellence, a willingness to submerge himself individually with a group effort, courage, an acceptance of pain and a love for what he is doing, respect for worthy adversaries and perhaps most importantly, the realization that not all in life can be success and victorious."

He called himself Johnny Blood and was Green Bay's most flamboyant Packer until Paul Hornung arrived years later. Known as the "Vagabond Halfback" for leapfrogging from team to team back in the 1920s, the eccentric John McNally was a free spirit off the field but a dedicated, innovative player on it. And a winner. After seeing a marquee promoting the Valentino movie, "Blood and Sand," he played pro ball under the name Johnny Blood in order to preserve his college eligibility. After teaming with iron man Ernie Nevers on the Duluth Eskimos during the mid-1920s, the colorful Blood-McNally took his racehorse speed and glue-fingered pass-catching skills to the Packers. He helped them win four world championships and combined with end Don Hutson to drive defenses crazy.

"Doug Atkins wasn't born," a sportswriter once said of the mastadon-like Bear defensive end.

Eccentric off the field but a brilliant runner and receiver, Johnny Blood McNally, top photo, leapfrogged from team to team. But some of his most productive and flamboyant years were with the great Green Bay Packer teams of the 1930s.

"Vince Lombardi did not invent professional football and he did not found the NFL, but he embellished both of them to a degree never surpassed and seldom, if ever, equalled. He made winners out of his players and losers out of his opponents."

—Wellington Mara

"The Arctic ice cracked, an explosion followed and he came out." At 6' 8" and 275 pounds, he was a Monster of the Midway who anchored the Bear line for 12 years and was an NFL starter for 17. Incredibly strong, he played with the zest of a rookie. A favorite tactic was to leap over crouched linemen and sack the quarterback. Atkins was one of those giants opponents learned not to upset. "Atkins aroused is a once-in-a-lifetime sight," a teammate remarked. "You see those crazy cowboy movies where the hero picks up guys in a bar-room brawl and throws 'em through walls? That's Atkins."

After a dispute with tight-fisted Bear owner George Halas over money, Atkins was traded to New Orleans in 1967. He played his heart out. In one game he went to the sideline and told the coach, "My leg feels funny." That night he was still walking around on it. After all, it was just a broken tibia.

Remarkably, Atkins is not the tallest Hall of Famer. That honor goes to 6' 9" tackle Bob St. Clair who spent 11 seasons in the trenches for the San Francisco 49ers.

Vince Lombardi, above, took the Green Bay Packers from doormats to dynasty, winning five NFL titles and two Super Bowls in nine years. He taught the basics, not razzle-dazzle. Gino Marchetti, right, was a tall, crashing defensive end for the Baltimore Colts. In 1969 he was chosen the best defensive end in the NFL's first 50 years.

Before Roger Staubach could be a field general for the Dallas Cowboys he had to finish his Navy duty. Staubach, famous for last-minute heroics, led the Cowboys to four titles and two Super Bowl wins.

They called Paul Hornung "the Golden Boy." When he came out of Notre Dame in 1957 as an All-America quarterback and glamorous Heisman Trophy winner, the sports world waited anxiously for more golden achievements at Green Bay. But the world had to wait until coach Vince Lombardi arrived in 1959 to transform the losing Pack into a dynasty and Hornung into a high-scoring halfback.

Hornung infuriated Lombardi with his late-night antics with fellow Casanova in cleats, end Max McGee. But Lombardi would later admit, "When the game is on the line, Paul Hornung is the greatest player I ever saw." Added teammate Bob Long: "Inside the 10-yard line he was probably the finest football player I've ever seen." Said McGee at Hornung's 1986 enshrinement, "He

didn't just run the ball, pass the ball and kick the ball. He blocked and for that his teammates as well as everybody in the country realize that he is one of the greatest all-around football players that maybe will ever play."

When Roger Staubach got to high school his coach wanted to switch him from end-halfback to quarterback. "I didn't want to do it," Staubach said. "I was an end. I was a running back and I wanted to really stick to being a receiver and he said, 'You are going to be a quarterback.' Well, that was the biggest decision in my life because I fought him on it, but he made me a quarterback and I have never regretted it."

At 275 pounds a true "Monster of the Midway" with the Chicago Bears, Doug Atkins, top photo, No. 81, went on to play defensive end for the New Orleans Saints with the zest of a rookie. "The Golden Boy," Paul Hornung, right, was a trial for Green Bay opponents as well as his coach, Vince Lombardi.

Brawny Bears, fullback Bronko Nagurski, above right, and end Bill Hewitt, upper left and inset, powered the Chicago offense in the 1930s. Durable Hewitt played without a helmet.

Named the 1963 Heisman Trophy winner while at the U.S. Naval Academy, Staubach faced years of active duty before he could play pro ball. Most teams refused to take a chance on him. Even Hall of Fame coach Tom Landry of the Dallas Cowboys admitted, "The odds were against him from the outset. The Cowboys drafted Roger as a future choice in the 10th round in 1964 when he still had a year in the Naval Academy and four years of active duty ahead of him. I never thought we would ever see this Heisman Trophy winner in a Cowboys' uniform. But when training camp opened in 1969 there was this 27-year-old rookie from Cincinnati and a navy haircut and a gung-ho attitude." Staubach was a player who "does not only possess outstanding athletic ability but has the inner qualities that make it just a joy to be around him," Landry told the enshrinement audience. "Twenty-three times he engineered fourth-quarter comeback victories, 14 of them in the final two minutes or in overtime."

During football's lean years of the 1930s, many players earned $100 a game or less, played 60 minutes a game and a few were so tough they refused to wear a helmet. One helmetless star was the Bears' legendary Bill Hewitt, a tough, cagy defensive end and tricky pass-catcher. A famous picture on display at the Hall of Fame shows him in action at the bitterly fought 1933 NFL Chicago Bears-New York Giants title game. With the Bears behind, 21-16, Bear fullback Bronko Nagurski faked a plunge, stopped short and flipped a pass to Hewitt. The picture shows the football in mid-air, just as the bare-headed Hewitt lateralled it to teammate Bill Karr. With tacklers closing in, Karr dashed through for the winning touchdown.

It was a Sunday in 1969 and just another 400-plus-yard passing day for Sonny Jurgensen. And he'd been sacked, pounded, flattened and battered behind another weak Washington Redskin line. But his coach, Vince Lombardi, told the press: "Sonny Jurgensen is a great quarterback. He may be the greatest this league has ever seen. He certainly is the best I have ever seen. He hangs in there in the worst of adversity. He is no longer a young man but he is all man. He will surely be in the Hall of Fame." Lombardi, as usual, was right on all counts. Redskin owner Edward Bennett Williams recalled a November day when the Skins were trailing the Cowboys 31-20 late in the game. An injured Jurgensen limped in to replace a hobbling Billy Kilmer and

"completed 11 straight passes for an impossible 34-31 victory."

Jurgensen scoffed at the quarterback-hero image. "In a team game, and football is the ultimate team game, everybody depends on one another, everybody contributes to the success." His high school coach, he told the enshrinement audience, had the key to winning. "He believed that character was the main ingredient."

"Nagurski is no mere name," Notre Dame "Four Horsemen" halfback Don Miller said at Bronko Nagurski's 1963 enshrinement. "It's an international way of saying football." When the Canadian-born fullback-tackle joined the Chicago Bears in 1930 from the University of Minnesota, he was solid as a tree at 6'2", 230 pounds and unstoppable as a bull. Some said he was small for a Ukrainian but before long, people were calling the Bears "The Monsters of the Midway," a section of Chicago where they practiced. Opponents couldn't figure out which was more punishing, trying to try to stop this juggernaut or suffering one of his back-breaking tackles. New York Giants center Johnny Dell Isola, playing against Nagurski for the first time, hurled himself into the hole just as Bronk hit it. "It was the hardest tackle I ever made," Isola recalled. "I remember saying to myself, 'I guess that will show you, Nagurski.' But as they were unpiling us, I heard the referee turn to the Bears and say, 'Second down and two.'"

Sonny Jurgensen, left, was a standout passer with the Philadelphia Eagles and Washington Redskins, although handicapped by injuries and weak teams.

Guess this Hall of Famer: In 1917 he played end for the Canton Bulldogs under an assumed name with Jim Thorpe. In 1919 he batted .357 for the Cincinnati Reds and met the infamous Chicago White Sox, later dubbed the "Black Sox," in the World Series. Called from the college coaching ranks to take over the doormat Philadelphia Eagles in the 1940s, he took them to two world championships in 1948 and 1949, led by Hall of Fame halfback Steve Van Buren. If you guessed Earle "Greasy" Neale, you're right.

When the Detroit Lions drafted Joe Schmidt as their seventh round pick in 1953, they felt he only had a so-so chance to make it. At 6 feet, 220 pounds he was marginal for a linebacker. Observed Lions owner William Clay Ford at Schmidt's 1973 enshrinement: "There are, however, qualities that certainly scouts or anybody who is drafting a ballplayer cannot measure: desire, leadership and courage. Nobody knew what quantity Joe had of these elements and Joe had tremendous quantities of these elements. He is probably one of the finest that has played middle linebacker. Nobody ever played it tougher."

Paul Warfield, a graceful, sure-handed receiver, was taught well by Ohio State coach Woody Hayes and went on to star with the Cleveland Browns and the great Miami Dolphins teams of the early 1970s. But at his 1983 enshrinement, Warfield had a message that went beyond football. "I think the lessons I have learned regarding character, sportsmanship and humility have come from the great coaches, they come from family and they have given me a sense, I believe, of commitment. Commitment to dedicate my ability as a player and commitment to strive for excellence. The vital lesson I think many of the athletes have learned is really no different than lessons that are learned in life itself.

"There are day-to-day struggles, there are times in which we fail, there are times in which we must learn to get up off the ground. Life is not going to be a smooth road. It is not going to be easy and consequently if you have that reserve from your experiences you can draw from, the chances are you will meet with success."

They said Jim Taylor, the man who put power into Vince Lombardi's Green Bay powerhouse

Fleet, sure-handed wide receiver Paul Warfield helped spark the undefeated Miami Dolphins during their Perfect Season of 1972.

widow, Marie Lombardi, said at Gregg's en-shrinement. "He was probably the finest all-around team player that has ever played this game." An All-Pro tackle, "he was perfectly willing to make the supreme sacrifice of switching from tackle to guard when he was needed," she said. "And to use the old cliches of honesty, integrity, commitment, excellence, dedication may sound old and tired but I don't know of any man who these apply to more than Forrest Gregg."

Gale Sayers, "magic in motion" as a broken-field runner with the Bears, had his brilliant career cut short by injuries. "Reaching this point," Sayers said at his 1977 enshrinement, "is not as important as striving to get here. This is true in all professions and all of life's activities. The most important thing is to strive to do our very best. Nothing is more of a waste than unrealized potential. As Robert Rawlings said, 'A man's reach should exceed his grasp.' If you should reach your goal, set new goals and strive for them. It is not enough to rest on yesterday's triumphs, but to continually strive for new goals and accomplishments."

teams, wasn't big enough to be a rock-em, sock-em fullback. But he was a rocklike 6 feet, 216 pounds. Said Lombardi: "Jim Taylor isn't big for a fullback but when you bump against him it's like bumping against an iron statue. In fact he likes that feeling." If Bart Starr's passing was the Packer lightning, Taylor was its thunder.

How many people know that Frank Gifford was All-Pro as a defensive halfback? True. That was during his early years as a two-way player with the New York Giants. During his great career Gifford made All-Pro three more times, then went on to more fame as a sports announcer. Gifford told the 1977 enshrinement audience about the value of working for a goal: "You don't always get there but sometimes when you strive hard enough what we do reach is better than the goal you set."

"Watching someone like Forrest Gregg work is like watching a great bullfighter or ballet dancer," Hall of Famer and Green Bay center Jim Ringo once observed. Gregg was a 6' 4", 250-pound tackle. "I read somewhere where Vince Lombardi made football players out of men and men out of football players, but not this man," the coach's

Handsome Frank Gifford, above left, was not only a high-scoring New York Giants runner and receiver but an All-Pro defensive back. Earle "Greasy" Neale, above, coached the once-doormat Philadelphia Eagles to championships in 1948-49.

Coach Paul Brown always said that Bill Willis was "the quickest down lineman in the history of football." Weighing only 215 as a middle defensive guard for the Cleveland Browns, Willis had to be fast. Where 300-pound bruisers used tank-like power, Willis employed finesse. An Ohio-born All-America for Brown at Ohio State, he was among those recruited when the coach was forming the Browns. "I have often said that Paul Brown saved my life," Willis said at his 1977 enshrinement "and if it had not been for him, I am certain that I would not be here receiving this honor today.

"Because it was he who afforded me the opportunity to play pro football when it was not the popular thing to do. I was the first black to play in the All-America Conference and Paul Brown arranged for me to play. I tell every young person that there is a formula for success. And that formula is to always do the very best you can with what you have wherever you are. And you will

find if you do the very best that you can, under any and all circumstances that the best will come back to you."

In 15 years with the New York Giants, center Mel Hein played in more than 200 games — offense and defense — and never missed one because of injury. As agile as he was durable, the 225-pound Hall of Famer was one of the few linebackers fast enough to cope with the great Green Bay Packer end Don Hutson. A fiercely aggressive tackler, Hein was hailed as a gentleman in a knee-and-gouge era.

At the Chicago College All-Star Game in 1965, most spectators saw a 260-pound raging bull of a

Small for a defensive lineman at 215 pounds, lightning-fast Bill Willis of the Cleveland Browns, No. 30, rushes Ram quarterback Bob Waterfield. When Dick Butkus, No. 51, opposite, rampaged at middle linebacker for the Bears, runners and quarterbacks lived in fear.

middle linebacker, Dick Butkus. But Chicago Bear coach George Halas, who had drafted Butkus, saw an overweight fellow Chicagoan and University of Illinois player. He told Butkus to shed 15 pounds in order to play pass defense well enough to be not just very good but great. Butkus obediently pared down to 245. "There are guys who make tackles and then there's Dick," said fellow linebacker Doug Buffone. "He's a mauler. I hit pretty hard but no matter how hard I hit I don't hit that hard." Quarterbacks lived in fear. "Butkus — if he doesn't tackle you himself you can hear him coming," said Terry Hanratty. "You know he's going to be there eventually. You have to be conscious of him. He has an instinct for the ball — passer, runner, anybody. It doesn't matter."

"Anyone who ever saw Dick Butkus play knows he was a superior football player," observed Pete Elliott, his coach at Illinois and executive director of the Pro Football Hall of Fame. "His tackling was devastating, his instincts were absolutely unbelieveable but the thing that sets him apart from every other athlete I have known is his great, great intensity. Dick played the game like it ought to be played, all out, all the time, every game, every practice. Dick Butkus is a yardstick, a yardstick for linebackers of all time."

When Vice President Gerald Ford, a former football player at the University of Michigan, spoke at the 1974 Hall of Fame ceremony, he laughed about a running joke by ex-President Lyndon Johnson. "Lyndon on more than one occasion would say that there was nothing wrong with Jerry Ford except that he played football too long without a helmet," Ford chuckled.

Football, Ford said, "gave me an opportunity to learn some of the basic lessons that you have to learn. And perhaps learn them with some disappointments and some accomplishments.

"But you learn them in cooperation with others. It is special because the players are typical Americans. They come from all segments of our society — rich, poor, north, south, east or west. It is an amelioration of the finest that I have seen in our total society."

Echoing Ford's comments, foreign-born Hall of Famer Leo Nomellini told his enshrinement audience: "Canton, Ohio, is thousands of miles from Lucca, Italy, where I was born. But Canton, Ohio, and the Hall of Fame are proof of what opportunity and sportsmanship in America really are."

Gridiron Victories

A pair of ice tongs. A cigar-scarred desk. A bench. A broken helmet. A warmup jacket dating to the 1930s. These are among the cherished mementoes that make the Hall of Fame professional football's great treasure chest.

Ardent fans who walk through the Hall's Enshrinee Mementoes Room have been known to get misty-eyed over a football signed by a championship team. Or yip in wonderment at the size of the giant high-top football shoes worn by the Bears' Bronko Nagurski.

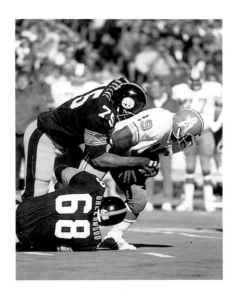

The ice tongs are just ordinary ones, dating to an era when footballs were fatter and many homes still cooled food with ice. But one of the most extraordinary runners in football history worked his way through school hauling 100-pound ice blocks with these tongs. Red Grange, "the Wheaton Iceman," took the job as a high school sophomore in Wheaton, Illinois, "because I needed the money." Grange's mother died when he was six. His father was a lumberjack who later became a Wheaton police chief.

"What it did, without me knowing it, was to develop my leg muscles," Grange said. "I mean I'd make about 50 calls a day on the average, up and down stairs with these huge blocks of ice, and it built my legs up." Even after he became a national sensation at the University of Illinois, the idol of millions, he returned home each summer to haul ice.

There are many helmets in the Enshrinee Mementoes Room but two of them tell especially dramatic tales. One has no facemask and the other is as shattered as the dreams of the man who wore it.

It reads like fiction. Backfield stars on the same high school team go separate ways to college.

Both win All-America honors. The fickle finger of football fate beckons them to the same pro team. There they become All-Pros and lead the club to NFL championships. As if these weren't honors enough, both are inducted into the Pro Football Hall of Fame.

The Texas twins, so different in temperament, were Bobby Layne and Doak Walker. The dark helmet with no face mask on display was worn by Layne, a blond, blue-eyed Texas boy wonder. Layne was tough as a longhorn steer and figured a mask would just get in his way throwing the football. When All-America Layne came out of the University of Texas in 1948, crafty George Halas acquired him for the Chicago Bears through a slick maneuver involving the Pittsburgh Steelers. But Halas, to his everlasting regret, let Layne slip away because he was loaded with quarterback talent in the form of the great Sid Luckman and Notre Dame star Johnny Lujack.

"Galloping Ghost" Red Grange worked his way through the University of Illinois hauling ice with tongs now displayed in the Enshrinee Mementoes Room. Bobby Layne, the tough Texan quarterback for the Detroit Lions and Pittsburgh Steelers, wore this helmet, above, but refused to use a face mask.

In Detroit, joined by high school teammate Doak Walker, Layne led the once-doormat Lions to three NFL titles in the 1950s. In the 1953 championship game, Layne's last-second TD pass and Walker's extra point beat Otto Graham and the Cleveland Browns, 17-16. A flamboyant lover of night life who gave $100 tips, Layne was the last quarterback to play without a facemask.

If there was a Jack Armstrong, the All-American Boy in the late 1940s, it would have been the Doaker. A three-time All-America at Southern Methodist and the 1948 Heisman Trophy winner, Doak Walker had movie-star good looks but the modesty of a choir boy. At 5' 11" and 173 pounds, Walker had great doubts that he'd make the pros. "Honestly," he said, "when I came into the Detroit training camp I expected to be on the first shipment home. My weight — or lack of it — bothered me." And Walker had no great compensating speed. Yet he could do everything well — run, pass, catch passes, run back kicks and even play defense if necessary. And he had a nose for the ball. As college coach Blair Cherry put it: "Uncanny ability to be in the right place at the right time, that was Doak's strong point."

Walker was an All-Pro four of his six years and won two NFL scoring titles. Out most of the 1952 season with an injury, Walker returned for the NFL Championship Game against the mighty Cleveland Browns of Paul Brown, Otto Graham and Co. With the Lions holding a slim 7-0 lead in the third quarter, quarterback Bobby Layne faked a pass, then handed the ball to the Doaker. He slipped through the line, cut to his left and ran 76 yards in the cold December afternoon of Cleveland and scored his only touchdown of the season. The Lions won.

When the same teams met again a year later for the NFL crown, Walker scored the first touchdown, booted a field goal and kicked two extra points as the Lions triumphed, 17-16. On display at the Hall of Fame is Doak Walker's kicking shoe, equipped with a zipper so he could speedily slip into it when points were needed.

In the NFL, if your name is Yelberton Abraham Tittle, you'd better be one heck of a football player. Tittle, a rawboned Texan, was.

But after 13 years as a pro — 10 with the San Francisco 49ers — few expected much when Tittle was traded to the New York Giants in 1961. Instead of being burned out, he sparked the Giants to three straight division titles. But all three times Tittle and the Giants were denied the NFL championship crown he had long cherished. The Giants lost the 1963 title game when the Bears beat him to a pulp and intercepted two of his passes for touchdowns. A tragic figure of frustration, the balding Tittle slammed his helmet onto the frozen turf, cracking the headgear. But Tittle won the respect of all and is now in the Hall of Fame. That split helmet is on display in the Hall of Fame's Enshrinee Mementoes Room.

Doak Walker and his touchdown twin from Texas, Bobby Layne, led the Detroit Lions to three NFL titles during the 1950s. The modest "Doaker," left, doubted that he could make the pros but the multi-talented halfback-kicker-receiver proved he could do everything well. Lions emblem is shown above.

A powerfully built lineman in a crouch looks out from a photo in the Giants' team display in the Hall. He looks like a tightly wound spring poised to flatten anyone foolish enough to get in the way. Steve Owen was a human dynamo who found in football a better life than the dusty Oklahoma Indian Territory where he was born. A 235-pound tackle when he broke in with the Kansas City Cowboys in 1924, Owen genuinely enjoyed the clashes of brute force that went on, play after play, in the line. He joined the Giants as a player in 1926 and coached them from 1931 until 1953. But he never forgot those football lessons in the pits.

"Football is a game played down in the dirt and always will be," he told those who thought his offenses old-fashioned. Considered a defensive genius, he won eight divisional titles and two NFL championships. The Giant-Bear clashes during the 1930s and 1940s were classic battles of gridiron titans. Yet a subtle mind was at work. Owen devised the vaunted "Umbrella Defense" against passes. When his injury-riddled Giants were losing to the Bears, 10-3, at halftime in the 1934 NFL title game, the crafty Owen shod the New Yorkers in sneakers. In the second half the Giants, with superior footing on the icy Polo Grounds field, raced over the Bears, 30-13.

Who was Earl "Dutch" Clark, whose warmup jacket hangs in a hallowed spot in the Detroit Lions team display? Back in the mid-1930s Clark was a superstar who shunned publicity. His brainy field generalship and jackrabbit-like running led the Lions to a smashing defeat of the New York Giants in the 1935 NFL title game. It was one of the few times any team broke the championship competition monopoly of the Giants-Bears-Packers during that decade.

One of the last of the triple-threat backfield stars and a brilliant, fast-thinking signal-caller, Clark was a deadly dropkick specialist. Although

not particularly fast afoot, Clark had instinctive open-field moves that led his coach, Potsy (no relation) Clark to remark: "He's like a rabbit in a brush heap." His 40-yard run in the 1935 title game broke the Giants' back. When the Pro Football Hall of Fame chose its first batch of inductees in 1963, Clark was among the charter members.

Fans still shake their heads over five straight games in 1970 when 43-year-old George Blanda's last-minute heroics averted sure defeat for his Oakland Raiders.

As long as football legends are told and men over 40 dream of glory, grizzled quarterback Blanda will be an inspiration. On October 25, 1970, he relieved Daryle Lamonica and threw three TDs and booted a field goal to sink Pittsburgh, 31-14.

A week later his 48-yard field goal with three seconds left tied Kansas City. In game three his last-second 52-yard field goal beat Cleveland. The following week Blanda tossed a touchdown to fellow Hall of Famer Fred Biletnikoff with 2:28 left to whip Denver. In the fifth game his field goal with seven seconds remaining left San Diego shocked and defeated.

Warmup jacket worn by the revered Detroit star of the 1930s, Earl "Dutch" Clark, hangs in the Lions' display at the Hall of Fame. Team displays such as the New York Giants, above, commemorate Hall of Fame enshrinees and the teams for which they played.

An inspiration to players and fans of all ages, quarterback George Blanda is best known for heroics in five straight 1970 games. Blanda, then 43, passed or kicked the Raiders to four last-minute wins and a tie. When he retired five seasons later he was the oldest player in NFL history.

It was a supreme year of glory for the son of a hard-working coal miner. One of 11 children, Blanda was brought up in the heart of western Pennsylvania's football country. His No. 16 jersey in the Hall of Fame harks back to a career that spanned 26 professional gridiron campaigns. When he retired from the Raiders for good in 1975 at the age of 48, no one else had ever played so long or at such advanced age or had survived 340 games. Blanda always said that he had three pro careers. The first started in 1949 as the Chicago Bears' unheralded 12th-round choice from Kentucky. His career, seemingly ended in 1958 when the Bears cut him loose, got new life in 1960 when the new American Football League desperately needed experienced quarterbacks.

But did they need a 33-year-old castoff? Blanda answered by leading the Houston Oilers to two AFL championships and very nearly a third. Then in 1967, Houston having decided his usefulness was at an end, Blanda was signed for a third career by the Raiders as a backup quarterback and kicker. Why not? After all, he wasn't quite 40.

"I was very proud of my heritage and I developed a lot of character in the early days in coal-mining country," Blanda told his 1981 Hall of Fame enshrinement audience. "I learned that through hard work, dedication and discipline and tenacity and never giving up, you can succeed in improving your life."

"Blanda knew how to lead, he knew how to win," Raiders chief Al Davis said. "I really believe

that George was the greatest clutch player that I have ever seen in the history of professional football."

Stop at the display showing O.J. Simpson's Buffalo Bills No. 32 jersey from his banner 1973 season. That was the year he slashed through and around NFL defenses for a record-breaking 2,003 yards. Simpson won four rushing titles for a Bills team that was not otherwise outstanding. How did he do it? At 212 pounds he was big but not a cannon-ball runner. He had great speed but NFL benches are full of fast backs. Simpson had something else, a shiftiness, a change of pace, a blinding acceleration that took him past the line of scrimmage and into the secondary, where he could make his moves. O.J. would glide and slide, then shift to overdrive.

Yet his first three seasons were ones of frustration and revolving-door coaching staffs. None of the coaches knew how to harness Simpson's great talents. Even great runners need the horses up front. Then coach Lou Saban arrived and put together an offensive line with the speed and strength to open holes for "The Juice." When Simpson was a boy in San Francisco, few would have guessed that a child with legs bowed from a rickets-like disorder that required him to wear braces would even become a sandlot athlete, much less go on to be a superstar with USC and the NFL.

What, you might ask, is an office desk — and a battered one at that — doing in a football museum? And look at it, covered with deep, dark scars from cigar butts left burning. But behind that desk sat NFL commissioner Bert Bell. When stogie-smoking Bell took over the job in 1946 the NFL had struggled through years of adversity and now was being threatened by the upstart All-America Football Conference. Bell steered the NFL from dark, red-ink days to the sunshine-bathed heights of postwar popularity and prosperity.

Bell was all too familiar with pro football's red ink as owner of the Philadelphia Eagles in the 1930s and co-owner of the Pittsburgh Steelers during the war years of the early 1940s. Bell starred at Penn after his father, who had played football there, assured friends that his son would go to Penn or nowhere! Both Bell and his desk went to the Hall of Fame, too.

It looks like something taken from an ordinary park, that bench in the Green Bay Packers team display. It's not. It's a players' bench used in the December 31, 1967 "Ice Bowl" NFL Championship Game at Lambeau Field, Green Bay — the last Vince Lombardi-coached game there.

On a frosty day when the mercury plunged to a minus 13 degrees and the wind-chill factor was worse yet, the Pack had to come back against the Dallas Cowboys. In a finish emblazoned in football history books, Hall of Fame quarterback Bart Starr followed a block by Jerry Kramer to sneak across the frozen turf in the last seconds for a 21-17 Packer win.

A shifty, elusive runner, O.J. Simpson, opposite, would glide and slide through the line, then shift to overdrive. Yet as a boy in San Francisco, a rickets-like disease required him to wear leg braces. Above, the Eagles team display.

Over at the Chicago Bears display, there's a small stool used by George Halas, the legendary Bears' owner who coached them for 40 years. The stool was on the sideline at Griffith Stadium, in Washington, D.C., when his Bears defeated the Redskins 73-0 for the 1940 NFL title.

Dried mud still clings to the cleats of the brilliant Bear halfback, George McAfee, whose football shoe is dwarfed by the neighboring cleats of the giant Bronko Nagurski. McAfee, a slim 177-pounder, was made for the T-formation, where his quick-openers slashed for big yardage. A racehorse broken-field runner, McAfee was also a brilliant defensive back. In the Bears never-to-be-forgotten 73-0 trouncing of the Washington Redskins in the 1940 championship game, McAfee intercepted a pass and ran it back for a touchdown. One opposing coach, Jock Sutherland, called him, "Frank Merriwell come to life." Just as his career peaked, McAfee left to spend four years in the service during World War II. But he came back strong after the war and in 1948 was the NFL punt return champion. After his playing days ended, McAfee returned to the playing field as an NFL official. When he was a high school gridder in Ironton, Ohio, his coach was Dick Gallagher, later director of the Hall of Fame, where McAfee was inducted in 1966.

Bronko Nagurski, on the other hand, was the very symbol of power. He weighed 225 and while bigger fullbacks came along none ever filled those monster boots the way Bronko did. While his bulldozing ball-carrying and punishing tackling have been acclaimed to the rooftops, many forget that his wrecking-ball blocking carved a black-and-blue path to many a touchdown. Grange

called him, "The greatest football player of all time." The story is told how Bronko knocked Philadelphia linebacker John "Bull" Lipski unconscious. Lipski went back into the game, tried to tackle Nagurski and was knocked out a second time. Two Philadelphia subs helped Lipski off the field but before they could, the Bears ran another play. Nagurski, leading the way, threw a block that sent all three of them flying. "Poor Lipski

Mementoes in the Hall include player bench from the last game Vince Lombardi coached at Green Bay, December 31, 1967. That was the "Ice Bowl," in which the Pack came back, rallying to beat Dallas for the NFL title.

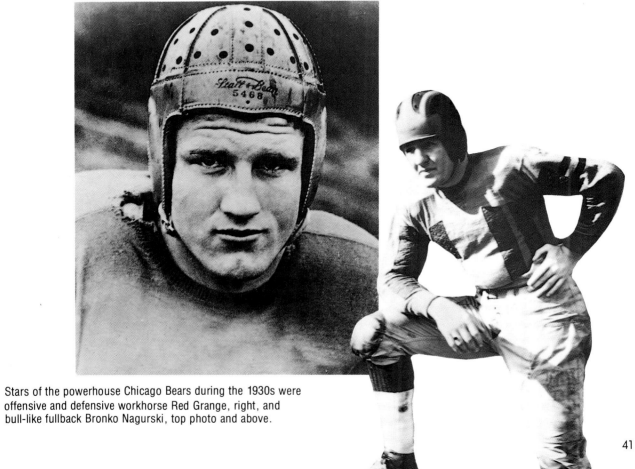

Stars of the powerhouse Chicago Bears during the 1930s were
offensive and defensive workhorse Red Grange, right, and
bull-like fullback Bronko Nagurski, top photo and above.

was knocked out for the third time," George Halas recalled, "A record that should stand until another Nagurski comes along, if one ever does."

Nagurski retired in 1937, but when the Bears ran short of players during the lean war year of 1943 Nagurski heeded the call. He played guard but when the Bears were losing to the crosstown rival Cardinals with a divisional title at stake, Nagurski took his old position at fullback. When he was finished, the Bears had a touchdown and went on to win. In the NFL Championship Game with the Redskins, Nagurski plunged for a TD to give the Bears the halftime lead. But even Nagurski couldn't keep Sammy Baugh from passing the Skins to a second-half win. In a sport obsessed with statistics, no one knows how many yards the Bronk gained because no one was counting during his first years.

Since being formed in Canton in 1920, the National Football League has been tested by numerous upstart leagues, the first of which was spearheaded by none other than Red Grange himself. Every new league blunted its green spear against the NFL fortress. Some say Grange's assault cost this gridiron warrior his legendary cutting ability. The story of these fledgling leagues is told in the Hall of Fame.

After Grange blazed a trail of headlines at the University of Illinois, his manager, "Cash and Carry" Pyle, arranged for him to join the Chicago Bears in 1925. Grange's barnstorming tour with the Bears captured public attention and helped legitimize the struggling, ragtag NFL. But after the tour Pyle demanded one-third ownership in the Bears for Grange to play the next year. Owner George Halas hit the ceiling and turned Pyle down flat. Denied a Grange-led New York NFL franchise to challenge the Giants, Pyle organized the American Football League. The AFL failed after the 1926 season but Pyle's New York Yankees, starring Grange, joined the NFL for the 1927 season. In a game with the Bears, Grange hurt his leg, robbing him of his broken-field speed and elusiveness. "After it happened, I was just another halfback," Grange said. Yet Grange rejoined the Bears in 1929 and in addition to his ball carrying became an outstanding defensive back until retiring after the 1934 season.

Rival quarterbacks in the titanic 1950 championship game were Otto Graham of the Cleveland Browns, top photo, and Bob Waterfield of the Los Angeles Rams, right. The Browns, newcomers to the NFL, beat the Rams, 30-28, and won new respect in the football world.

A second American Football League was formed in 1936 and a third in 1940. Each flopped after two seasons. But in 1946 the better-financed All-America Football Conference found fertile ground. And, with a host of players emerging from World War II duty, the AAFC had little trouble filling its ranks. One imaginative coach named Paul Brown gathered so much of this rich harvest and put it together so brilliantly that the Cleveland Browns were a powerhouse long after the AAFC merged with the NFL in 1950. Brown hired

star players from his coaching tour at Ohio State and his service team. There was the bruising 238-pound fullback Marion Motley, glue-fingered end Dante Lavelli, tackle and wonder-kicker Lou Groza and guard Bill Willis, all of whom made it to the Hall of Fame along with Brown himself. One of Brown's master strokes was selecting a single-wing halfback from Northwestern as his quarterback.

Otto Graham's passing was not only pinpoint but he threw a soft, easy-to-catch ball. With Graham as T-formation quarterback, the Browns so dominated the new league that they were champions all four years until the AAFC called it quits after 1949. With the Browns absorbed into the NFL in 1950, critics rubbed their hands. Now, they sneered, these minor leaguers would find out what it was like in the Big Leagues.

The Browns confounded critics by breezing to a 10-2 record, beating the New York Giants in the

playoffs and meeting the Los Angeles Rams for the title. It was virtually a Super Bowl 17 years early. The Rams were at their high-flying best, with a mighty offense starring Hall of Fame quarterbacks Bob Waterfield and Norm Van Brocklin throwing to Hall of Famers Elroy "Crazylegs" Hirsch and Tom Fears. No defense could contain this aerial circus.

But on December 24, 1950 the Californians had to cope with the wind howling off Lake Erie, frozen turf and 27-degree temperatures. Worse yet, Van Brocklin was out with a broken rib. Browns quarterback Otto Graham, on the other hand, lost the services of the always-reliable receiver Mac Speedie to a leg injury. But the loss was more than compensated for as Hall of Fame end Dante Lavelli turned in a brilliant performance.

Few defenses could contain the high-scoring aerial circus sported by the Los Angeles Rams of the 1950s. The Rams' brilliant ends were two Hall of Famers, Elroy "Crazylegs" Hirsch, above left, and Tom Fears, above. Passing to them were Bob Waterfield and Norm Van Brocklin, both also destined for Hall of Fame honors.

A field goal by Lou "The Toe" Groza was the margin of victory as the Cleveland Browns the Rams for their first NFL title in 1950. 250-pound Groza, above, also doubled as tackle. The Vince Lombardi Trophy, right, goes to the Super Bowl winner.

In the third quarter the lead seesawed as Cleveland pulled ahead, 20-14, and the Rams fought back to take the lead, 21-20. Then the Rams recovered a fumble by the usually reliable Marion Motley to forge to a 28-20 lead. With only minutes to play, Graham completed five straight passes to Lavelli and then hit Rex Bumgardner for the TD. When the Browns got the ball back, Graham passed and ran the ball to the Rams' 11. Only seconds remained. Then massive tackle Lou "The Toe" Groza kicked the field goal that gave the Browns a 30-28 victory. It also removed all doubt about whether they were big leaguers. Cleveland fans poured out onto the field in jubilation. After joining the NFL the Browns won seven divisional titles in eight years.

At 6' 3", 250 pounds and an alumnus of Ohio State, Groza was one of the original 1946 Browns. His football shoes, the right one squared off for kicking, are on display at the Hall of Fame, along with his complete uniform. After suffering a back injury in 1960, Groza limited himself solely to kicking until he retired in 1967, the last of the original Browns to do so.

In 1960 yet another rival, the American Football League, led by millionaire Lamar Hunt, a Hall of Famer, challenged the NFL. The AFL produced exciting football, new stars and gave new careers to NFL castoffs like George Blanda. The same critics that put down the AAFC called the AFL a bush league of second-raters. It took a brash youngster named Joe Namath to engineer one of the most dramatic upsets in sports history and reverse that verdict. First, the Super Bowl had to be invented. In 1966, the upstart AFL and the established NFL agreed to merge. They would play separate schedules until 1970 but meet in an annual championship game starting in 1967.

"In the AFL-NFL joint committee meetings, we had been referring to the 'final game,'" recalled Hunt, president of the Kansas City Chiefs. One owner wanted to call it the "Golden Game."

Recalled Hunt: "Sharron, my seven-year-old daughter, had a toy called a super ball. Subconsciously, I may have been thinking about Sharron's toy and one day I just happened to come out and call the game the 'Super Bowl.' Somehow or other the name just stuck." Visitors to the Hall of Fame will see a small red ball carefully sealed in clear plastic.

Whether it was the catchy name or the idea of the two superpowers of pro football clashing like gladiators, the game played January 15, 1967 caught the public's imagination as no other title game had. The AFL champion Kansas City Chiefs, with its monster line, gave the establishment NFL Packers lots of lip about the havoc they planned to wreak. On game day, Packer end Boyd Dowler was ailing and his place had to be taken by Max McGee, 34-year-old partying partner and touchdown twin of the flamboyant runner-kicker Paul Hornung. McGee had caught only three passes all year.

Yet the first score of the game was a 37-yard pass from quarterback Bart Starr to McGee. At halftime the Packers had only a slim 14-10 lead. But in the second half the Pack roared back like a fierce January storm over Green Bay.

McGee caught a 13-yard touchdown pass as Green Bay embarrassed the Chiefs, 35-10. McGee, the man who hadn't expected to play, finished the game with two TDs and caught seven passes for 138 yards. When the Packers beat the Oakland Raiders a year later in Super Bowl II, 33-14, many wondered if the AFL would ever win one. Joe Namath had no doubts.

Four days before Super Bowl III at the Orange Bowl in Miami January 12, 1969, Namath "guaranteed" that his New York Jets would beat the NFL's powerful Baltimore Colts. With the Colts 17-point favorites and pro football's best defensive team, this sounded brash indeed.

With quarterback Johnny Unitas sidelined most of the year with an elbow problem, Earl Morrall stepped in and did a masterful job. Colt coach Shula chose him to start the game over Unitas. Morrall had gotten them there. "Besides," Shula said, "I didn't feel that Unitas was 100 percent physically." Even so, Unitas was unhappy at not starting. The Colts may have been overconfident as they viewed the Jets' game films. "We didn't think they were really impressive," Shula said. "Their defense seemed awfully weak. It was tough showing these films to your squad and not having them get overconfident. The thing I tried to point out, but it evidently didn't sink in, was that Joe Namath was a great passer.

"During all of the time we were in Miami, there was the feeling that the AFL and its representative, the New York Jets, weren't qualified to play us in a Super Bowl and that it shouldn't be much of a game at all."

Meanwhile, crafty Jet coach Weeb Ewbank, a future Hall of Famer, had worked out a blocking scheme he felt would allow the Jets to run against the Colts. Jet fullback Matt Snell carried on the first two plays and crashed for a first down, proving Ewbank right. With Namath passing beautifully and Morrall being intercepted three times in the first half, the Jets pulled ahead.

Although Hall of Fame receiver Don Maynard didn't catch a pass that day, some insist that it was a pass he didn't catch that played a major role in the Jet victory. Early on, Namath aimed a 60-yard pass for Maynard that was just beyond his reach. With the Colts worried about the long bomb to Maynard, end George Sauer was left free to catch eight passes for 133 yards. In the second half, Unitas came off the bench to lead Baltimore to its only touchdown. Final score: Jets 16, Colts 7.

Keeping an eye on excellence, the Hall of Fame has a display for each Super Bowl, including the San Francisco 49ers' 38-16 win over the Miami Dolphins in Super Bowl XIX. After the NFL won the first two Super Bowls, Joe Namath led the AFL's New York Jets to a shocking upset over the NFL Colts.

Quick: How many touchdown passes did Namath throw that day? Answer: None. But he led the Jets to one of the greatest upsets in sports history. Except that the confident Jets didn't think it was an upset. The Jets went down in history, and Namath and Maynard won their place in the Hall of Fame.

The Kansas City Chiefs, again led by future Hall of Famers Len Dawson on offense and Willie Lanier, Bobby Bell and Buck Buchanan on defense, returned to the Super Bowl the next year and took revenge on the Minnesota Vikings. The AFL had evened the count with the NFL at two wins apiece and proved that its quality of play was on a par with the old pros.

No team ever had a better year than the Miami Dolphins did in 1972. Some predict that no club will ever again go undefeated, then win the Super Bowl. The Hall of Fame recaptures that startling achievement with its "Anatomy of a Perfect Season" in the Pro Football Adventure Room. Few would have predicted it. In 1970 coach Don Shula left the Baltimore Colts to take over a young Dolphin team that had never had a winning season. Its 1969 record was a dismal 3-10-1.

"Anatomy of a Perfect Season" exhibit counts milestones along the Miami Dolphins' undefeated year in 1972. In 1970 coach Don Shula took over a team that had never had a winning year. In three seasons they were unbeatable. Miami won every game in 1972, then beat the Redskins in the Super Bowl.

But a solid core of fine players awaited Shula's inspired coaching, including four future Hall of Famers, quarterback Bob Griese, fullback Larry Csonka, center Jim Langer and wide receiver Paul Warfield. In his first season, Shula lifted the Dolphins not only to a 10-4 record and second place in the American Football Conference's Eastern Division but a wild-card spot in the playoffs, where they were knocked off by the Oakland Raiders.

In 1971 the Dolphins won their division and soared into the Super Bowl, only to be badly whipped by a great Dallas Cowboys team led by Hall of Famer Roger Staubach. This defeat set the stage for the Perfect Season of 1972.

The Dolphins started fast, winning their first three games. Then came Joe Namath and the Jets, the Dolphins' arch rivals in the Eastern Division. Shula devised a shifting secondary aimed at confusing Namath. It worked, holding him to 152 yards. That made it four wins and no losses.

In the next game against the San Diego Chargers, Griese broke his leg when tackled trying to pass. Earl Morrall, who had not looked good in pre-season, trotted onto the field confidently and led the Dolphins to a 24-10 victory. With Morrall at the helm, and Csonka and Co. pounding out a record 2,960 yards on the ground, the Dolphins smashed their way through the entire schedule, winning all 14 regular season games. No NFL team had gone undefeated since the Chicago Bears won all 11 games in the World War II year of 1942.

Trailing Cleveland 14-13 with seven minutes left in the first playoff game, Miami forged ahead by blocking a punt for a TD. Then Morrall cooly moved the team 80 yards for a 20-14 win. Still, Shula was worried. Morrall was playing well but the team was having trouble moving the ball. Griese was recovered but Shula elected to start Morrall in the AFC Championship Game against the Pittsburgh Steelers, one of the emerging powerhouse teams of the 1970s. At halftime the score was tied, 7-7. But Morrall wasn't moving the team and Shula was forced to make a change.

It was a painful decision, benching a man who'd won 10 games during an undefeated season. But as the second half opened, Bob Griese was at quarterback. The Super Bowl was a prize not to be lost by indecision. The Steelers went ahead, 10-7 but Griese passed the Dolphins to a 21-17 win. Miami's record was 16-0. Only a Super Bowl victory over coach George Allen's "Over the Hill Gang" Washington Redskins stood between them and a perfect season.

No one wanted it more than the Dolphins' 235-pound fullback, Larry Csonka. He "was simply the best fullback of his time," Shula said. "He

was blood and guts and dirt all over him. In his career, high school, college and the pros, he had 12 broken noses. Csonka rushed for 8,061 yards in his career, but fumbled only 21 times."

On Super Bowl day in Los Angeles, the Dolphins were worried as they walked off the Memorial Coliseum field at halftime. They were only ahead 14-0, had blown at least one scoring chance and made other costly mistakes. They would have been scared out of their cleats if they'd known they were not to score another point in the game. In the second half, one of the most comic moments in Super Bowl history came when soccer-style kicker Garo Yepremian's field goal try was blocked by the Redskins. Yepremian picked it up on a bounce and shockingly tried to pass. The ball slipped from his grasp and flubbed through the afternoon sunshine. Redskin back Mike Bass caught it and raced 49 yards to one of the most improbable touchdowns in football history. But it wasn't funny to Shula. The score was 14-7 and the Dolphins had to be rattled by the bizarre twist of events. Washington got the ball back and with only seconds left on the clock quarterback

Long strides take the Miami Dolphins' fullback Larry Csonka, right, slashing past tacklers. Csonka, who helped power the unbeaten 1972 Dolphins, "was simply the best fullback of his time," according to coach Don Shula.

**Send this card
and enclosures to:**

"Pro Football Hall of Fame:
The Story Behind the Dream"
2121 George Halas Dr. NW
Canton, OH 44708

PRO FOOTBALL HALL OF FAME

ORDER FORM

Please send me_____ copies of "Pro Football Hall of Fame: The Story Behind the Dream" at $6.95 including postage. Payment enclosed.

Name

Address

City   State   Zip

_____ I'm also enclosing a check for _____ as my tax-deductible donation to support the non-profit Pro Football Hall of Fame.

Billy Kilmer faded back to pass for the tying touchdown. But he was engulfed by a tide of Dolphins. Miami won the Super Bowl and finished the year with an incredible 17-0 record. A perfect season!

Csonka, one of the many stars of that perfect team, fought back tears when he was enshrined in the Pro Football Hall of Fame in August, 1987. A native of nearby Stow, Ohio, he was inducted along with Dolphin center Jim Langer, who played every offensive down of that memorable 1972 season.

The 1970s produced three other dominant teams that sent its best and brightest players to the Pro Football Hall of Fame. The Dallas Cowboys, led by Hall of Fame coach Tom Landry, went to the Super Bowl five times in the decade. Two other future Hall of Famers for the Cowboys were rifle-armed Roger Staubach and defensive tackle Bob Lilly, who anchored the "Doomsday Defense."

The Pittsburgh Steelers scored four Super Bowl wins for Hall of Fame owner Art Rooney and coach Chuck Noll, thanks to the passing and running of Hall of Famers Terry Bradshaw and Franco Harris and defense of Hall of Famers Jack Ham, Joe Greene, Jack Lambert and Mel Blount. The Minnesota Vikings and cool-eyed coach Bud

Grant made it to the Super Bowl four times. Scrambling passer Fran Tarkenton went on to the Hall of Fame. The swarming defense featured Hall of Famer Alan Page and the "'Purple People Eaters."

The silver and black of the Oakland Raiders tyrannized opponents throughout the 1970s. Hall of Famers Fred Biletnikoff, Willie Brown, Gene Upshaw, Art Shell and Ted Hendricks each wear a Super Bowl XI ring as testimony to their teams' decade of excellence.

The Hall of Fame's bright display of Super Bowl rings is a glittering exhibit, but one sparkling ring was never worn by the man who earned it. After the Chicago Bears won the 1986 Super Bowl, a special ring was made for the late George Halas, longtime Bears owner who coached them for 40 years. Halas died in 1983 at the age of 88, before his dream of a Super Bowl victory came true.

Yet even rarer and perhaps more treasured than the Super Bowl memento is the Hall of Fame ring. Only the select few enshrined in pro football's house of heroes since it opened in 1963 can wear one. Halas, an NFL founding father, received one when he was in the 1963 charter class of enshrinees. That same year, Halas' Bears, led by

Bright prizes for victories won in bruising, black-and-blue struggle, diamond-crusted Super Bowl rings glitter in a display at the Hall of Fame, right. Defensive tackle Bob Lilly's No. 74 jersey, left, is a centerpiece of the Dallas Cowboys' team exhibit.

tight end Mike Ditka, defeated the New York Giants 14-10 and claimed the NFL title. This would be Halas' last championship team, but for Ditka, just another step closer to his 1988 enshrinement. The largest ring, size 19 1/2 was made for Bronko Nagurski.

In the modern era of great players like Jim Brown, O.J. Simpson, Walter Payton and Eric Dickerson, it seems incredible that from 1934 through 1945 no blacks were seen on NFL playing fields. A thought-provoking display at the Hall of Fame tells the story of "The Black Man in Pro Football." It portrays some of the blacks who pioneered in the pros before and after the National Football League was formed in Canton in 1920. And even before blacks disappeared from the playing fields after 1933 as though swept by an invisible hand, they had to suffer racial insults.

It may come as a surprise to many that Paul Robeson, a Walter Camp All-America end and Phi Beta Kappa at Rutgers, played in the pros before turning to the stage as a singer and actor. Robeson, 6'3" and 217 pounds, played end for Akron, Ohio, and Milwaukee, Wisconsin for two years in the 1920s.

One of the best known of the black pros was Frederick Douglass "Fritz" Pollard, a star at another Eastern college, Brown. A halfback, he played with Akron, Milwaukee, Providence and Hammond, Indiana, where he joined his teammate from Brown, end Jay "Inky" Williams. Pollard was also the first black NFL coach. Pollard coached not only one NFL team but three, the Milwaukee Badgers, the Hammond Pros and Akron Pros during the early and mid-1920s.

Probably the most famous of the early black athletes was the racehorse tackle, Duke Slater. After playing at the University of Iowa, Slater joined the Chicago Cardinals and became an NFL all-pro, playing for 10 years. Red Grange called him "the greatest tackle of all time."

Other blacks played in the NFL but suddenly, after 1933, the music stopped. Some claim that club owners made a "gentlemen's agreement" to no longer sign blacks.

From 1934 until the post-war year of 1946, black players vanished from the NFL playing fields. This forgotten chapter of gridiron history is spelled out in the Hall of Fame exhibit portraying "The Black Man in Pro Football."

by years of semi-pro football. Ironically, his 1939 running mate at UCLA, Jackie Robinson, broke the color line in major league baseball, joining the Brooklyn Dodgers in 1947. Soon after Washington's signing in early 1946 the Rams also hired the second black player of the modern era, Woody Strode. The 31-year-old former UCLA end had been a teammate of Washington and Robinson. Strode became Washington's roommate on the Rams.

Although Washington and Strode were trailblazers, two other blacks, signed a few months later in 1946 by coach Paul Brown of the fledgling All-America Football Conference's Cleveland franchise, made a far greater impact. That's because the two Rams only flashed briefly on the pro scene while Marion Motley and Bill Willis became enduring stars of Paul Brown's great Cleveland Browns dynasty. In 1946 they were the only blacks in the AAFC but they led

Breaking pro football's color line in 1946 were two former UCLA teammates, runner Kenny Washington, top photo, and end Woody Strode, left. Both trailblazers were signed by the Los Angeles Rams, newly moved from Cleveland. The same season the Cleveland Browns signed two blacks who would become stars in the great Browns dynasty, fullback Marion Motley and lineman Bill Willis.

the way for many more to follow in both leagues. Warned by Brown that they would face abuse, they kept their tempers and won respect from opponents. At 238 pounds, Motley, a former high school standout in Canton, became the prototype giant fullback of the modern era. He was a rock-solid blocker who protected passer Otto Graham and confounded opponents with lightning speed when hitting the line on trap plays. Yet Motley was equally valuable as a punishing tackler and highly mobile linebacker. Willis, an All-America at Ohio State when Brown coached there, weighed only 215 but was so fast and aggressive as a two-way guard that he dominated AAFC opponents and went on to become an all-pro in the NFL. Today, both Motley and Willis are enshrined in the Pro Football Hall of Fame.

Pioneer pros included halfback Fritz Pollard, right, the first black pro coach, and Duke Slater, above, All-Pro Chicago Cardinals tackle. Browns Hall of Fame guard Bill Willis, No. 30, opposite, was one of the first blacks signed after World War II.

Evolution of the Pro Football Hall of Fame

*T*he Pro Football Hall of Fame is a dream that was built into reality by contributors like the Canton police who kicked in a dollar apiece.

And workers who pitched in 50 cents each when it counted. And donors like the insurance agent who pledged $300 in 1962 and made faithful $6.25 monthly payments for years, even after he'd moved away.

A steelworkers' union collected $5,000. One company gave a 25-ton air conditioner. But the single most important donation was $100,000 from the Timken Roller Bearing Co. That made the NFL chieftains sit up and take notice of little Canton's bold bid for the Hall of Fame.

Records of those 1962 community donations from the high and the humble, hundreds of meticulously kept donor cards in neat handwriting, are still in the Hall of Fame. But if it hadn't been for the Canton Repository, Executive Editor Clayton Horn, and a small Middle America town with spirit, the Hall of Fame today might be in Detroit, Green Bay, Los Angeles or Latrobe, Pennsylvania. Latrobe? Well, it seems that in 1947, based on a since-disproved belief that the town near Pittsburgh had the first paid player, in 1895, the NFL awarded the Hall of Fame honor to Latrobe. But the town never got it off the ground.

When Canton started running with the ball in the early 1960s those other cities went on offense too. But it was too late. Canton was ahead.

Canton was a natural for the Hall of Fame site. It had been a cradle of pro football back in its rag-tag days in the early 1900s. Jim Thorpe had his glory days after joining the Canton Bulldogs in 1915. And the NFL itself was formed in 1920 when men from 11 teams met in Ralph Hay's Hupmobile showroom in Canton, bringing relative order out of chaos. The Bulldogs were powers in the young NFL, winning two straight championships in 1922-23.

On January 30, 1952, the people of Canton, at a dinner attended by more than 700 admiring fans, paid tribute to Jim Thorpe. Included were several of Thorpe's former Bulldog teammates who reminisced with and about the great Indian athlete. This event kept the community's connection with and enthusiasm for pro football alive.

The spark that lit Canton's enthusiasm to create a football shrine was an electrifying headline in the Canton Repository on Sunday, December 6, 1959: "Pro football needs a Hall of Fame and logical site is here." The blazing banner head topped

a challenging story by sportswriter Chuck Such. H.H. Timken Jr., the steel company's board chairman, read the story and accepted the challenge. He put the company squarely behind the dream. Canton community leaders promptly mounted a grass-roots campaign.

They were ready when NFL owners met in early 1961. William E. Umstattd, a Timken executive, and others arrived with a scale model of the proposed Hall. The Hall, he told the NFL owners,

A towering figure in the NFL, Tim Mara, above, gave pro football a big boost and a New York home in 1925. Far-sighted Mara had never seen a game but paid $2,500 for a franchise in Manhattan. The Giants were to become a major power in the young NFL as well as a big-city cornerstone. At left, NFL Commissioner Pete Rozelle, also a Hall of Famer, greets Billy Sullivan, long-time owner of the New England Patriots.

NFL Commissioner Pete Rozelle.

"He set up an office consisting of two small rooms in the Onesto Hotel in Canton and began the job of sorting out the memorabilia of the fastest growing game in American sports.

"He called it 'going from the Redskins to Jim Thorpe.'" Rozelle wielded a silver shovel at groundbreaking ceremonies on August 11, 1962. More than a year later, on September 7, 1963, the Hall of Fame opened and 17 charter members were enshrined. "These are the milestone men of pro football," McCann said.

The pioneers included a meat packing plant employee who bought the Green Bay franchise for $50, a rich bookie who founded the New York Giants and a wet-wash magnate whose vision led to rule changes in the 1930s that opened up the passing game.

would cost about $350,000 to build. Timken would contribute $100,000 and the people of Canton would donate another $250,000, he said. Impressed, the NFL sent a committee spearheaded by Paul Brown of the Cleveland Browns, who'd coached at nearby Massillon High School; George Halas, owner of the Chicago Bears and one of the pioneers who'd come to Canton in 1920 to form the NFL; Edwin Anderson, owner of the Detroit Lions; and Art Rooney, owner of the Pittsburgh Steelers. Even former players, like Link Lyman of the Canton Bulldogs and Chicago Bears, campaigned for Canton by contacting the committee members to voice their support. In April, 1961, NFL owners voted to award the Hall of Fame to Canton.

The Ohio town kicked off its building fund drive in December, 1961 and exactly two months later pledges reached $378,026. With a park-like setting as the site, the Hall of Fame needed only the driving force of a bundle of energy named Richard McCann, who became the Hall's executive director in April, 1962.

"Dick McCann left his job as general manager of the Washington Redskins in 1962 to become the director of the Hall of Fame at a time when it was little more than a hole in the ground," recalled

It was in the Canton auto showroom of Ralph Hay, above, that pioneer pro football leaders met in 1920 to form what is now the NFL. Before that, pro football was disorganized. Hay was manager of the Canton Bulldogs. Joe Carr, top left, was president of the NFL from 1921 until his death in 1939, leading the pros from sandlots to stadiums.

Milestone man Curly Lambeau was born in little Green Bay, Wisconsin, starred as a high school passer and played one year, 1918, at Notre Dame for Knute Rockne. A year later, working at a Green Bay packing company, he talked the owner into sponsoring a football team. Two years later Lambeau scrounged up $50 for a franchise in the NFL. Lambeau played for, then coached, the Packers for 31 years, then went on to coach the Chicago Cardinals and Washington Redskins.

Tim Mara was born on New York's tough lower East Side and had to hustle for a living. A lad with a quick mind for figures, Mara struck it rich as a bookmaker during the Roaring 1920s. In 1925, by sheer chance, he met Joe Carr, a former Ohio sports editor who had taken over from Jim Thorpe as president of the fledgling National Football League. Most NFL teams were in small Midwestern tank-towns and Carr badly needed a franchise in the Big Apple. Mara had never seen a football game but promptly wrote out a $2,500 check. "A New York franchise to operate anything ought to be worth $2,500," he reasoned.

George Marshall was a laundry tycoon in Washington, D.C. but a showman at heart. In 1932, Carr talked Marshall and three other men into starting an NFL team in Boston. When Beantown responded even to winning teams with a giant yawn, an infuriated Marshall moved the team to Washington, where it remains. Rules he helped push through in the 1930s changed pro football from dreary head-butting contests to a razzle-dazzle, wide-open game that drew larger and larger crowds.

Each year Canton honors new Hall enshrinees at "Football's Greatest Weekend." The Festival Parade is watched by 200,000 people. The Hall of Fame Game at Canton after the enshrinement ceremony traditionally kicks off the NFL preseason.

The 1963 charter class of Hall of Fame enshrinees also included Marshall's star quarterback, "Slingin Sammy" Baugh, former NFL commissioner Bert Bell, Joe Carr, Detroit Lions triple-threat star Dutch Clark, Chicago Bear immortal Red Grange, pro football's human cornerstone George Halas, Giant center Mel Hein, old-time Canton lineman Pete Henry, Green Bay's mammoth tackle Cal Hubbard, Packer end par excellence Don Hutson, Green Bay speedster runner and pass-catcher Johnny Blood McNally, Bear fullback Bronko Nagurski, iron man do-everything Ernie Nevers of the Duluth Eskimos and Chicago Cardinals and Jim Thorpe himself.

Since its 1963 opening, the Hall of Fame has inducted at least three professional football greats every year and hosted millions of fans from every state and scores of foreign countries. In 1971 it dedicated a $620,000 expansion, opened a $1,200,000 second expansion in 1978 and unveiled a $250,000 refurbishing in 1983.

The Hall is more than a museum and proud showplace. Its library-research center holds in its files the history of professional football in its thousands of photographs, game programs and

books, plus miles of film. It's a place where sports scholars do research. There is also a large movie theater, gallery of prize-winning game photos and supermarket-size store.

In 1988 the Hall of Fame celebrated its 25th anniversary. Its marriage with Canton and a world of football fans is clearly working.

Each year the new enshrinees are hailed at an extravaganza dubbed "Football's Greatest Weekend." It's part national gridiron lovefest and part county fair. The Hall of Fame Game series traditionally kicks off the NFL preseason and draws capacity crowds to Fawcett Stadium, just punting distance from the Hall. About 40,000 gather in downtown Canton to munch at the Ribs Burnoff and over 200,000 turn out for the fireworks show and concert. Thousands attend the Mayor's Breakfast and Fashion Show Luncheon. The Enshrinees Civic Dinner attracts more than 3,000, which is far more than the attendance at many early NFL games. Hot air balloon fests and drum and bugle competition add to the excitement and color.

Enshrinees, toughened players all, have confessed that they've choked up at the overwhelming welcome they get at the Festival Parade, watched by over 200,000 people. And they've been known to break down and cry at the Enshrinement Ceremonies on the Hall of Fame steps attended by up to 10,000 people. With their families and friends in the audience and NFL players and coaches on hand to recall their deeds, this is an occasion of high emotion and sentiment

"Football's Greatest Weekend" in Canton also includes the Hall of Fame Festival Balloon Classic, with dozens of hot air balloons lifting off daily. They rise from Weis Park and fill the sky with a rainbow of color.

for the enshrinees. Then, fittingly, it's time for football and the traditional Hall of Fame Game that kicks off another NFL preseason.

The Hall, launched under the guidance of executive director Dick McCann, who died in 1967, gained momentum under successor Dick Gallagher and continues to flourish under Pete Elliott, who before accepting the Hall of Fame post was a successful college coach and backfield coach of the St. Louis Cardinals.

Hall of Famers are selected by a board comprised of one media representative from each NFL city, (two from New York and Los Angeles because they have two teams each) plus one from the Pro Football Writers Association and one member-at-large. They meet at Super Bowl time to make selections from a list of finalists. The fans themselves can suggest candidates for the original list of candidates by writing to the Hall of Fame. A player must have been retired at least five years to be considered and coaches must no longer be active.

Each enshrinee has his own bronze bust and niche in the Hall, but even before then he has won a place in the fans' hearts. Without them there would be no pro football.

And perhaps there would be no Hall of Fame at Canton without a man named Jack Cusack. A young gas company clerk, he managed the Bulldogs and was inspired to hire Jim Thorpe to play in 1915. Cusack's master stroke helped make the team a powerhouse. And Thorpe's magic name went far in legitimizing a tainted, rough-house sport many top collegians shunned upon graduation. When you see Thorpe's bronze statue in the Hall's lobby, think of Cusack. He donated it.

There's an "I'll never quit" spirit that runs as a common bond among enshrinees. It's a bold spirit that lives on in the Hall of Fame, along with Canton's special brand of Middle America pride, the kind that built the Hall of Fame.

Breaking ground for the Pro Football Hall of Fame in Canton on August 11, 1962. Harry Stuhldreher, left, one of Notre Dame's Four Horsemen players of the 1920s, beams as NFL Commissioner Pete Rozelle mans the shovel.

62

HERE'S TO THE MILLIONS OF FANS WHO ARE, HAVE BEEN AND WILL ALWAYS BE THE LIFEBLOOD OF PRO FOOTBALL
. . . NFL COMMISSIONER PETE ROZELLE

Herb Adderley	Dick Butkus	Daniel J. Fortmann, M.D.	Bill Hewitt	Yale Lary
Lance Alworth	Tony Canadeo	Frank Gatski	Clarke Hinkle	Dante Lavelli
Doug Atkins	Joe Carr	Bill George	Elroy (Crazylegs) Hirsch	Bobby Layne
Morris (Red) Badgro	Guy Chamberlin	Frank Gifford	Paul Hornung	Alphonse (Tuffy) Leem
Cliff Battles	Jack Christiansen	Sid Gillman	Ken Houston	Bob Lilly
Sammy Baugh	Earl (Dutch) Clark	Otto Graham	Robert (Cal) Hubbard	Vince Lombardi
Chuck Bednarik	George Connor	Harold (Red) Grange	Sam Huff	Sid Luckman
Bert Bell	Jimmy Conzelman	Joe Greene	Lamar Hunt	William Roy (Link) Lyn
Bobby Bell	Larry Csonka	Forrest Gregg	Don Hutson	Tim Mara
Raymond Berry	Willie Davis	Bob Griese	John Henry Johnson	Gino Marchetti
Charles W. Bidwell, Sr.	Len Dawson	Lou Groza	David (Deacon) Jones	George Preston Marsh
Fred Biletnikoff	Mike Ditka	Joe Guyon	Sonny Jurgensen	Ollie Matson
George Blanda	Art Donovan	George Halas	Walt Kiesling	Don Maynard
Mel Blount	John (Paddy) Driscoll	Jack Ham	Frank (Bruiser) Kinard	George McAfee
Terry Bradshaw	Bill Dudley	Franco Harris	Earl (Curly) Lambeau	Mike McCormack
Jim Brown	Albert Glen (Turk) Edwards	Ed Healey	Jack Lambert	Hugh McElhenny
Paul E. Brown	Weeb Ewbank	Mel Hein	Tom Landry	John (Blood) McNally
Roosevelt Brown	Tom Fears	Ted Hendricks	Richard (Night Train) Lane	August (Mike) Michals
Willie Brown	Ray Flaherty	Wilbur (Pete) Henry	Jim Langer	Wayne Millner
Buck Buchanan	Leonard (Len) Ford	Arnie Herber	Willie Lanier	Bobby Mitchell